Name	Wishes and Comments

Name	Wishes and Comments

Name	Wishes and Comments

Name	Wishes and Comments

Name | Wishes and Comments

Name | Wishes and Comments

Name | Wishes and Comments

Name | Wishes and Comments

Name	Wishes and Comments

Name	Wishes and Comments

Name	Wishes and Comments

Name	Wishes and Comments

Name	Wishes and Comments

Name	Wishes and Comments

Name	Wishes and Comments

Name	Wishes and Comments

Name	Wishes and Comments

Name	Wishes and Comments

Name	Wishes and Comments

Name	Wishes and Comments

Name	Wishes and Comments

Name	Wishes and Comments

Name	Wishes and Comments

Name	Wishes and Comments

Name	Wishes and Comments

Name	Wishes and Comments

Name	Wishes and Comments

Name	Wishes and Comments

Name	Wishes and Comments

Name	Wishes and Comments

Name	Wishes and Comments

Name	Wishes and Comments

Name	Wishes and Comments

Name	Wishes and Comments

Name	Wishes and Comments

Name	Wishes and Comments

Name	Wishes and Comments

Name	Wishes and Comments

Name	Wishes and Comments

Name	Wishes and Comments

Name

Wishes and Comments

Name

Wishes and Comments

Name

Wishes and Comments

Name

Wishes and Comments

Name	Wishes and Comments

Name	Wishes and Comments

Name	Wishes and Comments

Name	Wishes and Comments

Name	Wishes and Comments

Name	Wishes and Comments

Name	Wishes and Comments

Name	Wishes and Comments

Name	Wishes and Comments

Name	Wishes and Comments

Name	Wishes and Comments

Name	Wishes and Comments

Name	Wishes and Comments

Name	Wishes and Comments

Name	Wishes and Comments

Name	Wishes and Comments

Name	Wishes and Comments

Name	Wishes and Comments

Name	Wishes and Comments

Name	Wishes and Comments

Name	Wishes and Comments

Name	Wishes and Comments

Name	Wishes and Comments

Name	Wishes and Comments

Name	Wishes and Comments

Name	Wishes and Comments

Name	Wishes and Comments

Name	Wishes and Comments

Name	Wishes and Comments

Name	Wishes and Comments

Name	Wishes and Comments

Name	Wishes and Comments

Name

Wishes and Comments

Name

Wishes and Comments

Name

Wishes and Comments

Name

Wishes and Comments

Name	Wishes and Comments

Name	Wishes and Comments

Name	Wishes and Comments

Name	Wishes and Comments

Name	Wishes and Comments

Name	Wishes and Comments

Name	Wishes and Comments

Name	Wishes and Comments

Name	Wishes and Comments

Name	Wishes and Comments

Name	Wishes and Comments

Name	Wishes and Comments

Name	Wishes and Comments

Name	Wishes and Comments

Name	Wishes and Comments

Name	Wishes and Comments

Name	Wishes and Comments

Name	Wishes and Comments

Name	Wishes and Comments

Name	Wishes and Comments

Name	Wishes and Comments

Name	Wishes and Comments

Name	Wishes and Comments

Name	Wishes and Comments

Name	Wishes and Comments

Name	Wishes and Comments

Name	Wishes and Comments

Name	Wishes and Comments

Name	Wishes and Comments

Name	Wishes and Comments

Name	Wishes and Comments

Name	Wishes and Comments

Name	Wishes and Comments

Name	Wishes and Comments

Name	Wishes and Comments

Name	Wishes and Comments

Name	Wishes and Comments

Name	Wishes and Comments

Name	Wishes and Comments

Name	Wishes and Comments

Name	Wishes and Comments

Name	Wishes and Comments

Name	Wishes and Comments

Name	Wishes and Comments

Name	Wishes and Comments

Name	Wishes and Comments

Name	Wishes and Comments

Name	Wishes and Comments

Name	Wishes and Comments

Name	Wishes and Comments

Name	Wishes and Comments

Name	Wishes and Comments

Name	Wishes and Comments

Name	Wishes and Comments

Name	Wishes and Comments

Name	Wishes and Comments

Name   Wishes and Comments

Name   Wishes and Comments

Name   Wishes and Comments

Name   Wishes and Comments

Name	Wishes and Comments

Name	Wishes and Comments

Name	Wishes and Comments

Name	Wishes and Comments

Name	Wishes and Comments

Name	Wishes and Comments

Name	Wishes and Comments

Name	Wishes and Comments

Name	Wishes and Comments

Name	Wishes and Comments

Name	Wishes and Comments

Name	Wishes and Comments

Name	Wishes and Comments
Name	Wishes and Comments
Name	Wishes and Comments
Name	Wishes and Comments

Name	Wishes and Comments

Name	Wishes and Comments

Name	Wishes and Comments

Name	Wishes and Comments

Name	Wishes and Comments

Name	Wishes and Comments

Name	Wishes and Comments

Name	Wishes and Comments

Name	Wishes and Comments

Name	Wishes and Comments

Name	Wishes and Comments

Name	Wishes and Comments

Name	Wishes and Comments

Name	Wishes and Comments

Name	Wishes and Comments

Name	Wishes and Comments

Name	Wishes and Comments

Name	Wishes and Comments

Name	Wishes and Comments

Name	Wishes and Comments

Name	Wishes and Comments

Name	Wishes and Comments

Name	Wishes and Comments

Name	Wishes and Comments

Name   Wishes and Comments

Name   Wishes and Comments

Name   Wishes and Comments

Name   Wishes and Comments

Name | Wishes and Comments

Name | Wishes and Comments

Name | Wishes and Comments

Name | Wishes and Comments

Name	Wishes and Comments

Name	Wishes and Comments

Name	Wishes and Comments

Name	Wishes and Comments

Name	Wishes and Comments

Name	Wishes and Comments

Name	Wishes and Comments

Name	Wishes and Comments

Name	Wishes and Comments

Name	Wishes and Comments

Name	Wishes and Comments

Name	Wishes and Comments

Name	Wishes and Comments

Name	Wishes and Comments

Name	Wishes and Comments

Name	Wishes and Comments

Name	Wishes and Comments

Name	Wishes and Comments

Name	Wishes and Comments

Name	Wishes and Comments

Name

Wishes and Comments

Name

Wishes and Comments

Name

Wishes and Comments

Name

Wishes and Comments

Name	Wishes and Comments

Name	Wishes and Comments

Name	Wishes and Comments

Name	Wishes and Comments

Name	Wishes and Comments

Name	Wishes and Comments

Name	Wishes and Comments

Name	Wishes and Comments

Name	Wishes and Comments

Name	Wishes and Comments

Name	Wishes and Comments

Name	Wishes and Comments

Name

Wishes and Comments

Name

Wishes and Comments

Name

Wishes and Comments

Name

Wishes and Comments

Name   Wishes and Comments

Name   Wishes and Comments

Name   Wishes and Comments

Name   Wishes and Comments

Name	Wishes and Comments

Name	Wishes and Comments

Name	Wishes and Comments

Name	Wishes and Comments

Name

Wishes and Comments

Name

Wishes and Comments

Name

Wishes and Comments

Name

Wishes and Comments

Name   Wishes and Comments

Name   Wishes and Comments

Name   Wishes and Comments

Name   Wishes and Comments

Name

Wishes and Comments

Name

Wishes and Comments

Name

Wishes and Comments

Name

Wishes and Comments

Name	Wishes and Comments

Name	Wishes and Comments

Name	Wishes and Comments

Name	Wishes and Comments

Name | Wishes and Comments

Name | Wishes and Comments

Name | Wishes and Comments

Name | Wishes and Comments

Name   Wishes and Comments

Name   Wishes and Comments

Name   Wishes and Comments

Name   Wishes and Comments

Name	Wishes and Comments

Name	Wishes and Comments

Name	Wishes and Comments

Name	Wishes and Comments

Name	Wishes and Comments

Name	Wishes and Comments

Name	Wishes and Comments

Name	Wishes and Comments

Name | Wishes and Comments

Name | Wishes and Comments

Name | Wishes and Comments

Name | Wishes and Comments

Name   Wishes and Comments

Name   Wishes and Comments

Name   Wishes and Comments

Name   Wishes and Comments